W9-CXN-685

LEARN ABOUT

Whales and Sharks

Edited by Belinda Gallagher
Cover design by Oxprint Ltd.

ISBN 0 86112 687 4

Published by Brimax Books Ltd, Newmarket, England 1991.
Second printing 1991.
Printed in Hong Kong.

LEARN ABOUT

Whales and Sharks

Written by Jane and David Glover
Illustrated by Brian Watson

Brimax · Newmarket · England

Whales live in the sea but they are not fish. They are mammals like seals and dogs. They cannot breathe underwater like fish, so they must come to the surface to fill their lungs with air.

The biggest whales are the blue whale and the fin whale. They are huge – much bigger than any dinosaur.

Dolphins and porpoises are smaller whales, about 10–30 feet (3–10m) long.

Whales are very intelligent. They live together in families and take great care of their young.

Sharks are fish. Instead of lungs they have gills, so they can breathe underwater. Inside, instead of bones, they have a tough rubbery cord called cartilage. Sharks are not as intelligent as whales.

The blue whale is the biggest animal that has ever lived. An adult can be 100 feet (30m) long and weigh as much as five trucks. Even a new born blue whale calf is heavier than an elephant and drinks 130 gallons of its mother's milk a day.

Big whales need to eat several tons of food a day. But they don't hunt big prey – they feed on some of the smallest plants and animals in the sea.

The bowhead whale swims along with its mouth open catching millions of tiny plants and animals called plankton. Instead of teeth, it has strips of whale bone in its mouth that act as a sieve. The whale moves its tongue to force out the water leaving the food behind.

Grey whales spend the summer feeding in the cold arctic ocean around the north pole. They suck up worms and shellfish from the mud on the sea floor. In the autumn they travel thousands of miles south to have their young in the warm waters off California and Mexico.

The mothers keep a careful watch on their babies. One mother is known to have fought off several killer whales, holding her calf out of reach with her flipper.

Big whales used to be much more common than they are now. Man hunted them with harpoons for their meat, whalebone and oil. They killed so many that some species nearly disappeared. Fortunately, most countries have now banned whale hunting, so numbers are increasing again.

Some whales have proper teeth and hunt larger prey than plankton and shellfish.

The sperm whale is the biggest toothed whale. It hunts giant squid which live deep in the ocean. It can hold its breath for over an hour as it dives down hundreds of feet to feed. When it surfaces it breathes out through the blowhole on top of its head, sending a jet of spray high into the air.

Killer whales are the fiercest hunters in the sea. They feed on seals, penguins, fish and other whales – but they have never been known to attack a human. Up to twenty killer whales hunt together in a pack called a 'pod'.

Belugas and narwhals are small toothed whales that live in the arctic. They feed on fish, crabs and shrimps.

Male narwhals are the only whales with a tusk. The tusk is a special tooth that grows into a spiral more than 7 feet (2m) long.

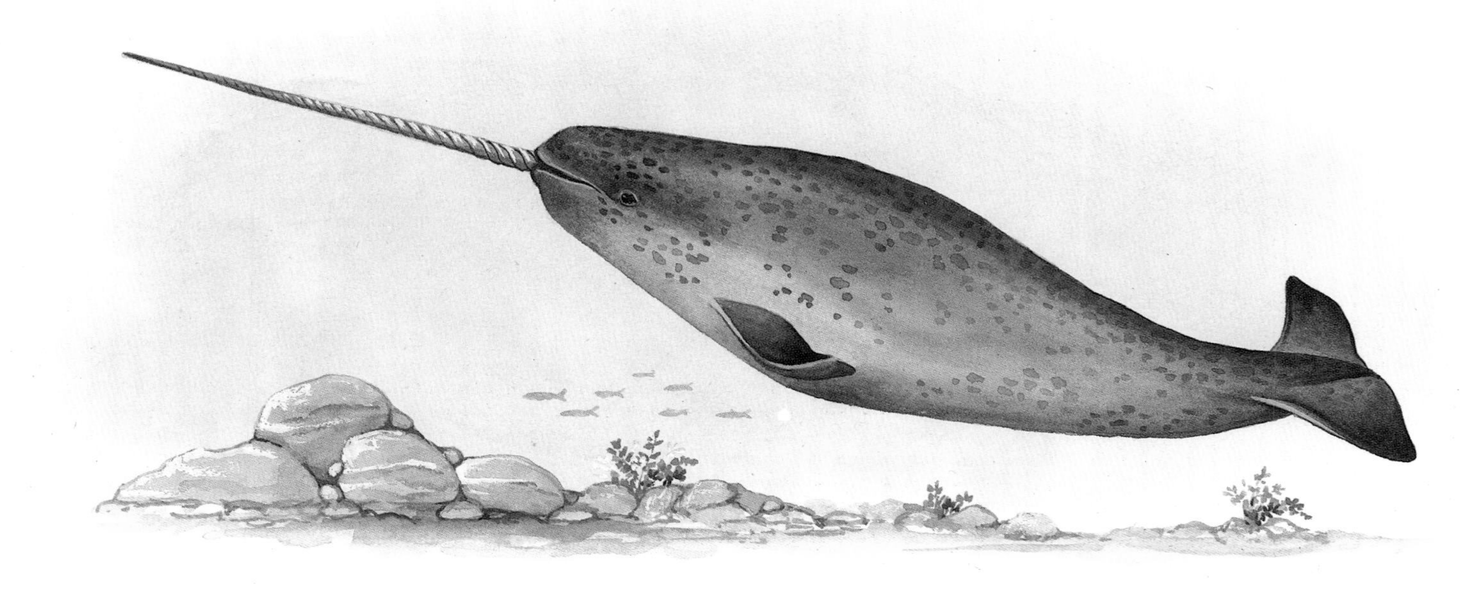

New born belugas are grey but as they grow they become paler until they are pure white. Beluga families are often seen swimming along in single file with the mother at the head. Like other whales they are noisy – talking to each other with a complicated language of sound. Sailors call belugas 'sea canaries' because of their loud 'singing'.

The Ganges river dolphin has become almost blind. The river water is so muddy, it finds fish by making sounds and listening for echoes – just like a bat.

There are more than 30 kinds of dolphin in the oceans and rivers. They are all superb swimmers.

Common dolphins swim together in large groups called schools, leaping high out of the water as they play and fish. If one is injured then others help it to the surface to breathe.

When a bottlenose dolphin has her baby, several females gather around to protect her. As the calf grows an aunt helps the mother to take care of it.

Baby sharks hatch from eggs. Some mothers keep the eggs inside their bodies until they hatch. Others lay them in special cases and leave them clinging to weeds. After they have hatched the babies receive no care from their parents – they must look after themselves.

Not all sharks are dangerous. The two biggest sharks are quite harmless. They eat plankton like the giant baleen whales.

The whale shark is the biggest fish in the world. It can be 60 feet (18m) long and weigh 13 tons. It lives alone, swimming slowly near the surface sieving plankton from the water. Basking sharks lead similar lives.

The great white shark is common in warm seas. It is very dangerous and attacks anything it thinks is food, including people. Sharks cannot see very well but they have a very good sense of smell. They can smell blood in the water from a great distance.

The white shark's teeth are sharp and jagged for cutting its prey. If its front teeth are broken, new ones grow from behind to replace them.

The hammerhead is another dangerous shark. No one really knows why its head is such a funny shape. It may be that having widely spaced nostrils and eyes help it decide where food can be found.

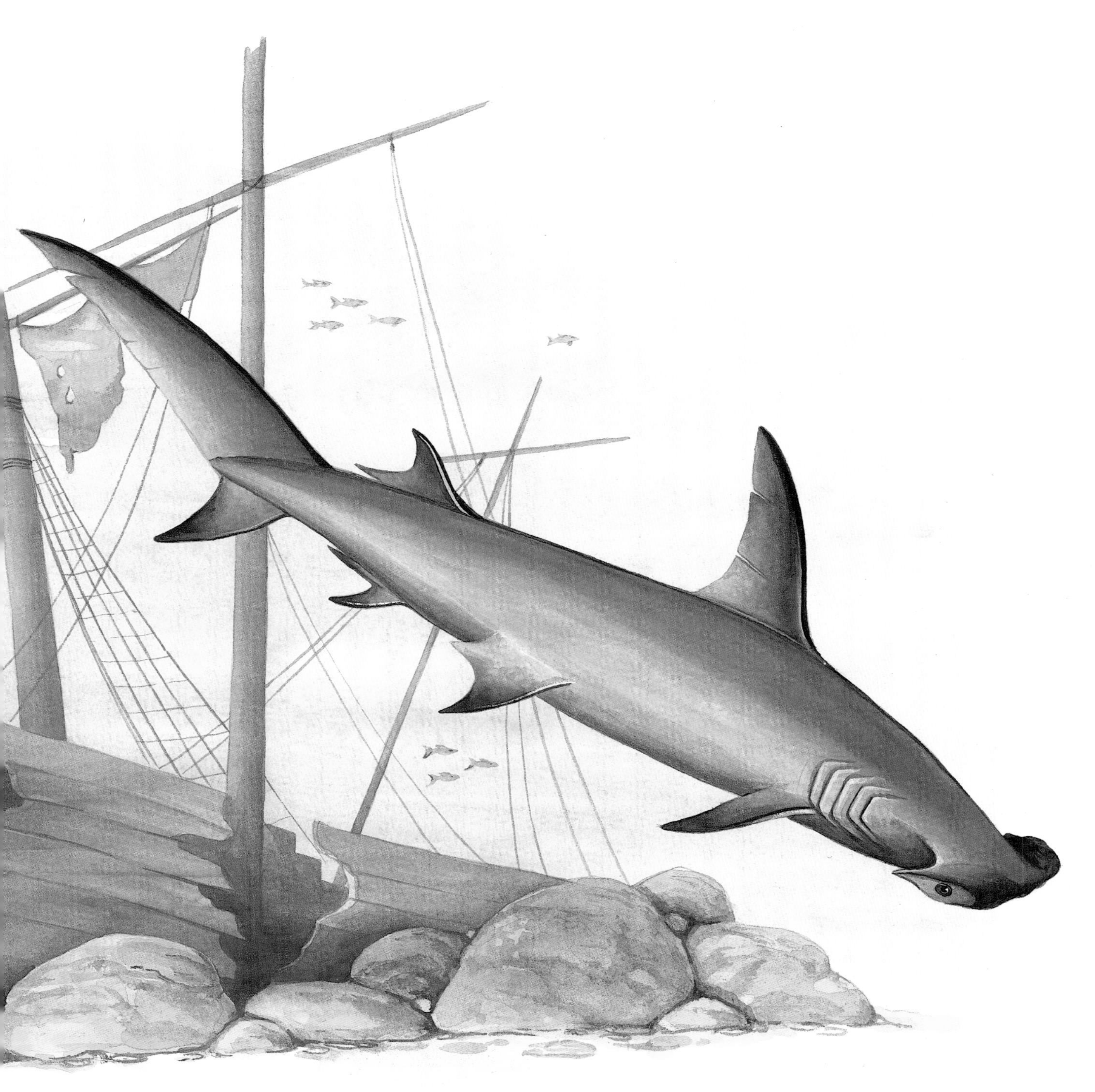

Thresher sharks hunt in groups. They splash the water with their long tails to trap a shoal of fish. They do not attack people.

Dogfish are small sharks that live in shallow water around the coast. They eat fish, shellfish and shrimps. You can often find their egg cases on the beach. Like other sharks, dogfish have very rough skin. Carpenters sometimes use it as a kind of sandpaper.

The wobbegong is a strange shark that lives on the sea bottom around Australia. The frills around its head make it difficult to spot amongst the weeds as it lies in wait for its prey.

Whales and Sharks quiz

Now you have read about whales and sharks how many of these questions can you answer? Look back in the book for help if you need to.

True or false?

1. Whales are fish.
2. Grey whales breed in the arctic.
3. Killer whales don't attack people.
4. Sharks are more intelligent than whales.
5. Dogfish are small sharks.

Odd one out

Which is the odd one out and why?

6. beluga narwhal wobbegong

7. blue whale sperm whale fin whale

8. white shark whale shark basking shark

Answers

1. False – whales are mammals.
2. False – they travel south to warmer waters to breed.
3. True
4. False – whales are much more intelligent than sharks.
5. True
6. Wobbegong – it is a shark, the others are whales.
7. Sperm whale – it is a toothed whale, the others are baleen whales.
8. White shark – it is a dangerous hunter, the others eat plankton and are harmless.